Jarrold Tree Series
With text by **Roland E. Randall**

Trees in Britain
Broadleaved Book 3

Jarrold Colour Publications, Norwich

Many people think of trees as a separate group of plants. In fact a tree is only a woody perennial plant which grows taller and thicker year by year. 'Tree' is really a word of convenience that has no strict botanical meaning. Usually, though, we think of trees as being unbranched for some distance above the ground and as growing to a height of over 20 ft (6–7 m). Shorter plants that are still woody but are branched near the ground are shrubs. However, in good environmental conditions many shrubs will grow to 20 ft (6·5 m) and in harsh conditions some trees will grow only 2–3 in (6–7 cm) above ground level.

The Broadleaved trees are distributed widely among the families of flowering plants that make up our British flora. Some families like the Maples (Aceraceae) include only trees and shrubs; others like the Spurges (Euphorbeaceae) are herbs in Britain but include trees in other parts of the world. Families like the Roses (Rosaceae) include trees, shrubs, and herbs in Britain.

Many plant species include varieties which occur in certain ecological conditions or in certain localities. Some of these can be very difficult to identify. Among the British trees this problem is acute among the Elms (Ulmaceae) and there are other species such as the Willows (*Salix* species) where hybrid forms are common and identification is therefore awkward. Conversely, the trees of each genus are usually very characteristic and identification to that level is easy.

Latin botanical names are included in this booklet because of the precision in description and their international acceptance. The generic name is written first followed by the specific name for example *Fraxinus excelsior*, the Common Ash. This species is in no way related to the Mountain Ash (*Sorbus aucuparia*), which is in fact, a member of the Rose family. After the specific adjective the name (or abbreviation) of the original publisher of the name is given. Sometimes there is a double citation if a later author has transferred the species to another genus. The final information is the maximum height of the species in Britain.

It is a severe problem to know which species to include in a book of British trees. Silver Birch, Scots Pine, Common Oak, Yew, for instance, have been with us since the retreat of the glaciers, whereas Sycamore, Norway Spruce, or Sweet Chestnut are not native, in the sense that centuries ago man introduced them. Those eventually selected for this series are the trees that are more commonly found in town or country outside specialised parks and gardens.

The importance of trees in our landscape is not usually appreciated until they are felled. Both in town and country trees are one of the most significant landscape features. Trees not only add beauty to our landscape but they are also vitally important in creating a suitable environment for other plants and animals. Trees are host plants to many forms of life from mosses and lichens to insects, birds and mammals. Native species like the Oak and the Ash are particularly important in this respect. That is why at a time when new mechanised farming methods are reducing our hedgerows, the Nature Conservancy is encouraging native tree-planting.

This booklet is one in a series which describes trees commonly found in Britain. Here some of the Broadleaved trees are described. The other booklets deal with the Conifers and their allies and further Broadleaved trees.

I would like to thank the following persons or bodies for permission to include photographs of trees on their property: Norfolk Naturalists Trust, Norwich Corporation, Dr E. A. Ellis, Cambridge University, Maurice Mason, Lord Hastings, John Last, and others unknown.

Most of the Broadleaved trees are deciduous, shedding their leaves in winter, though there are exceptions like the Evergreen Oaks and Holly. This means that many other characteristics must be used for identification at other times of the year: bark, buds, flowers, and fruit. Form is rarely of great use for identification because this will vary according to environment. In summer identification is fairly easy because there is usually foliage and either flower or fruit; in autumn the leaves will often be a different colour and ripe fruits may be present; in winter there will only be doubtful form, bark, twig, and bud to assist, but in spring there will be a new flush of leaves often again different in colour and size from the summer crop.

Arrangement of winter buds may be alternate as in Beech, opposite as in Ash or spiral as in Pedunculate Oak. The buds themselves can be many different colours and shapes and may be hairy as Hazel or sticky as Horse Chestnut. The arrangement of leaves follows that of the buds. The leaves may be simple as Birch or compound as Ash and may vary in shape from linear in Willows to triangular as most Poplars. Leaf margins may be entire, wavy, lobed, or toothed, the surface may be hairy or hairless and the colour may vary above and below. Some leaves have long stalks and others are virtually stalkless. Flowers can often help a great deal in naming trees in spring because some Broadleaved trees bear only one sex of flower and others are hermaphrodite. The variety of flower is huge from the catkin of the Willow to the huge spike of the Horse Chestnut. Bark is often a useful characteristic, but it must be remembered that most species have a thin, green, smooth bark when they are young and only attain their typical bark at maturity. Trees like Beech retain their smooth bark for life, but Elm becomes deeply furrowed and Oak becomes cubed. The colour of some barks is often the result of lichens growing on them and this can easily confuse.

The families described in this booklet include Magnolia, Pea, Dogwood, Elm, Mulberry, Olive, Elder. Also covered are the woody climbers and some smaller native and alien trees. They are mostly insect-pollinated species and thus many flowers are showy. Much seed-dispersal is aided by wildlife, thus fruits are often bright or edible. On the other hand Ash and Elm are good examples of wind-dispersed species. The Magnolia family comprises trees of Asia and America that were more widespread millions of years ago. The Pea family is one of the larger floral taxa having representatives in all non-Polar areas. Their main advantage is that the roots carry nodules which are the homes of symbiotic nitrogen-fixing bacteria. This enables them to colonise very poor soils. The flowers are composed of 5 petals, 3 forming a keel and 2 wings. The fruit is a pod or legume. The Elms are part of a family that includes Zelkovas in Eurasia and Hackberries in North America. The Elms occur east of the Rockies and north of the Himalayas. In all species the flowers come before the leaves and the fruit has a wing to aid dispersal. Leaves are often variable on any one tree and identification should be made from those of short shoots rather than from those of suckers or long new shoots. The Mulberry family, including Figs, is part of a large tropical taxon. The species that we see in this country very rarely naturalise. The Olive family, including Ash, Lilac, Privet and many garden shrubs, is not large, but is very widespread. Most have opposite leaves. The Elder family is mainly north-temperate in distribution. The species all have hermaphrodite flowers, most of which are highly attractive to insects, and most have a berry or drupe fruit. There are few wooded places in this country which do not contain one or more of the species described.

1 **BLADDER-NUT** *Staphylea pinnata* L. 20 ft
2 **SPINDLE** *Euonymus europaeus* L. 25 ft

The **Bladder-Nut** is a shrub that has been introduced from
central and southern Europe and planted in shrubberies of
southern England. From there it has escaped into the wild and
naturalised in a few places, sometimes reaching tree-like proportions. Bladder-Nut has opposite compound leaves with
5–7 finely toothed leaflets that are from 2 in. to 4 in. in length.
The small white flowers (1b) hang in a terminal cluster 2–5 in.
long. The strange fruits are the most obvious feature of this
species (1c) as they are an inflated membranous capsule like a
small whitish-green football about 1·5 in. across. These fruits,
which develop in July–August have 2–3 ribs along the surface. Both at flower and fruit stages they are very attractive to
butterflies and other insects. Individual stems never get very
large (1a) and are smooth olive-green with many ivory lenticels.
The **Spindle** is an important but generally inconspicuous
native tree that is found over much of England, Wales and
Ireland especially where the soil is lime-rich. The tree gets its
name from the fact that its extremely hard, smooth-grained
white wood was used for spindles in the days before the
spinning wheel was invented. For most of the year the Spindle
goes unnoticed because it has dark-green twigs and curious
greenish-yellow flowers (2b) that blend with the foliage within

1a

1b

1c

2a

2b

which the tree is growing. These flowers unfold in May–June, each having 4 petals, 4 sepals, 4 stamens and a 2-celled ovary. Flowers of some trees have only rudimentary anthers, others have an infertile pistil, such that effectively one gets male and female individuals. They are pollinated by many small insects. The distinctive fruits which make Spindle so beautiful develop from the female flowers into a 4-lobed pink or scarlet berry enveloped into a fleshy orange aril (2a). When the seed-capsule opens the seeds are suspended for a time on the long seed-string. The leaves are opposite and lance-shaped with fine teeth and blue-green undersides. When crushed they have an unpleasant smell and were once dried to make louse-powder. In autumn the leaves turn first yellow, then deep red. The smooth grey to pale-brown bark (2c) and the leaves are poisonous and the fruit is a purgative and emetic. It is the only northern European tree which contains the horny gutta-percha in its bark. The small ermine moth often makes its home on Spindle trees and it is the winter host of the bean aphis. For the latter reason many trees have been cut down over the last thirty years.

2c

3 TULIP-TREE *Liriodendron tulipifera* L. 100 ft
4 MAGNOLIA, CUCUMBER TREE *Magnolia acuminata* L. 60 ft

3a

3b

3c

In North America, where it is native, the **Tulip-Tree** is an important timber producer, the wood being called poplar (in U.S.A.) or canary whitewood (when imported to Britain). In Britain it is a hardy fast-growing tree once over 3–4 ft high, but it is only planted as an ornamental. The Tulip-Tree and its relative the Magnolia are very ancient species dating back to the Cretaceous period with a very primitive flower structure. The tree was introduced to England about 1650 and there are now many magnificent specimens in old parks and gardens. The buds and leaves of the Tulip-Tree (3a) are peculiar. Each bud is enclosed in a pair of large stipules. As the outer pair open they release a folded leaf and inside there is another bud and another leaf. Each leaf is about 5 in. wide, with sharply pointed lobes and a concave apex into which the midrib projects as a bristle. The leaf-stalk is slender and angled so that the leaf quivers. The bark (3b) is grey and furrowed in an even, shallow

4a

4b

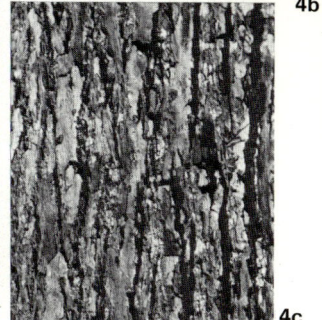
4c

network. The flowers (3c) only develop in this country in very hot summers. They have 3 large green reflexed sepals and 6 petals which are orange at the base and pale green at the tip. Inside there are a mass of stamens and long anthers. Occasionally cone-like fruits about 2 in. across develop and the winged seeds may germinate the next spring.

Many species of **Magnolia** are grown as ornamentals, some being introduced from North America and some from Asia. *M. soulangiana* (4b) with its beautiful early spring flowers is one of the commonest in British gardens but this only grows as a large shrub. More magnificent as a tree is the Cucumber Tree which was introduced from America in 1736 and is now found in many parks and gardens. This species has a rich orange, brown and purple bark (4c) narrowly furrowed into vertical ridges. It is a long-lived tree but does not have the beautiful flower of the Asian shrub species. The leaves are large, up to 10 in. by 6 in., and elliptic with crinkled margins. The flowers are bell-shaped, greenish yellow (4a) but rather insignificant, growing to about 3 in. high in midsummer. This species gets the name Cucumber Tree from the erect fruits which develop in autumn. These are bright-pink 'cucumber'-shaped 'cones' which ripen to a deep red (4d).

4d

Although another introduced species, the **Laburnum** freely sets seed in Britain and may occasionally be found as a sapling or seedling in hedgerows and woodland edges. It was a very early import from central Europe and is common in small gardens and city parks alike. The bark (5c) is a very distinctive smooth dark green, becoming patterned pale brown with orange flakes and transverse clefts as the tree gets older. Even though it is a small tree, the dark-brown heartwood and yellow sapwood are important in the production of musical instruments. The leaves grow on long stalks with 3 leaflets that are grey-green above and silky below. The flowers and fruit immediately identify this tree as a member of the Pea family. The flowers, each about 1 in. long are bright yellow and hang in racemes up to 10 in. in length (5a). The seed pods are 3 in. long, slender and twisted (5b), becoming dark brown in autumn. The small black seeds contain cytisin and are highly poisonous. Like all members of the Pea family the roots support nodules which contain nitrogen-fixing bacteria which aid the tree in its food supply. As a rule this tree is rather short-lived. Two other Laburnums may be seen: Scotch Laburnum which has larger leaves and does not flower till late June (a month behind the common species) and the hybrid Voss's Laburnum which is the best to plant in gardens because it rarely produces the poisonous seeds.

5a

5b

5c

5 LABURNUM, GOLDEN RAIN *Laburnum anagyroides* Medic. 20 ft
6 ACACIA, FALSE ACACIA, LOCUST TREE *Robinia pseudoacacia* L. 90 ft

6a

6b

6c

The **Acacia** was imported from North America early in the seventeenth century when there were hopes of it becoming a highly important timber tree. Its greeny-yellow wood is hard, tough and durable, but in this country it is not frost-hardy and rarely grows a straight form. The tree is very distinctive with its domed crown and it has been planted extensively as a screen around such things as coal tips, where the nitrogen-fixing bacteria help improve the soil quality. The grey bark is rough and deeply fissured with spiral furrows (6c). This species has attractive compound leaves (6b) that unfold late in the season, usually mid-May. They are composed of 7–19 sub-opposite, oval leaflets about 1·5 in. long, light green on the upper surface and blue-green below. The typical white peaflowers hang in racemes much like Laburnum (6a) and are rich in nectar. The 10-seeded pods ripen to a dark grey-brown and often remain on the tree long after its leaves have fallen. The tree obtained its Latin name in honour of Robin the French gardener who first planted it in Europe. Locust Tree arises from confusion with the tree from which John the Baptist obtained locust-beans in the wilderness.

7 JUDAS TREE *Cercis siliquastrum* L. 35 ft
8 LONDON PLANE *Platanus × hybrida* Brot. 100 ft

7a 7b

7c

The **Judas Tree** is a pleasantly shaped small tree that comes from the Mediterranean region, but has been grown in the southern parts of Britain since the mid-seventeenth century. It grows very slowly and older trees are usually sloping with branches curving up from ground-level. The bark (7c) is virtually black with numerous fine brown fissures. Shoots are dark red-brown, with lenticels. The long-stalked leaves are alternate, smooth and kidney-shaped about 3 in. by 4 in., yellow-green above and blue-green below. They tend to fall early in the autumn. The flowers (7a) are gorgeous rose-purple clusters looking rather like sweet-peas. They develop in mid-May from old leaf-scars or from very dwarf shoots, almost directly on the bole. Often the tree is a mass of flower before the leaves open. The fruit is a pod about 4 in. long with 10–14 seeds (7b), purple in summer, becoming brown and remaining on the tree till midwinter. White-flowered versions of this beautiful tree are very occasionally met with. It will grow on virtually all but the heaviest soils but does not naturalise.

8a 8b

8c

The **London Plane** is a hybrid between the Oriental Plane, *P. orientalis* and the American Plane, *P. occidentalis*, neither of which grow well in Britain. These species are part of a very ancient genus which developed in the Cretaceous period. London Planes were introduced to Britain in the seventeenth century and they were found to grow exceptionally well especially in urban areas (8b). Town smoke is resisted by the ability of the tree to shed bark at intervals, so keeping open its pores. In fact the bark (8a) is one of the most easily recognisable parts of the tree, being smooth, dark grey and brown with large whitish-yellow and green patches having thin peeling edges. Often there are fine vertical fissures and folds. The boles of some trees are heavily burred. The lobed leaves closely resemble those of Maples but they can be simply distinguished by the fact that they grow alternately. Leaves are variable in size up to 8 in. by 10 in. and when young are covered with down that produces bronchial upsets with some people. The inflorescence are catkins with 2–6 flower-heads; yellow male and crimson female flowers growing on separate catkins. The developed fruits cluster to form a ball almost 1 in. across hanging on a stem about 3 in. long. These brown bobbles remain on the leafless trees throughout the winter. Only occasionally are they fertile but self-sown seedlings sometimes occur on urban wasteground. These, too, are distinctive (8c) as there are strap-shaped crescentic seed-leaves and an unlobed first true leaf. Trees grow fast and live to a great age. The timber, lacewood, is valuable for high-class furniture and it may well become an important trimber crop. Today its main use is as an ornamental because it is so tolerant of poor soil, impure air and lopping.

9 MISTLETOE *Viscum album* L.

10 DOGWOOD *Swida sanguinea* Opiz 20 ft

Mistletoe is included in this booklet because it is a woody, evergreen parasite that grows on the branches of trees. In Britain it rarely grows in great enough quantities on any one tree to do any harm. Mistletoe grows on many different species of tree but is most commonly found on Apple, Poplar, Hawthorn (9b) and Lime. It is unusual to find it on evergreens and never on conifers. Mistletoe grows in most counties of England and Wales but it prefers to parasitise trees growing on calcareous soils. The branches are green and forked and the leaves are 2–3 in. long, yellow-green, opposite, narrow and leathery. Mistletoe has separate male and female plants. The flowers are small and inconspicuous, growing in April–May in clusters of 3–5 at the end of branches (9c). Male flowers have 4–6 white petals, female flowers have 4. The fruits, which develop in early winter (9a), are ivory, shiny berries about the size of large peas, with 1 or 2 black seeds. The berries contain sticky flesh which makes them adhere to birds' beaks and they are thus distributed to other trees. When the

9a

9b

9c

10a

10b

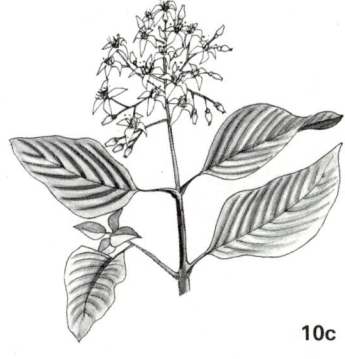

10c

seeds germinate a stem develops which grows into a crack on the bark; from this roots penetrate between bark and wood. From early times Mistletoe has been associated with magic and superstition and it is now the traditional 'kissing branch' of Christmas.

Dogwood is a name locally given to many of the smaller trees from which wooden skewers, or 'dogs' were made. However, the true Dogwood is a distinctive small tree or bush that is shot through with blood-coloured pigment in both leaves and twigs. It is most frequently found growing on chalk but it turns up almost anywhere south of the Scottish Highlands where the soils are lime-rich. Often Dogwood occurs in hedgerow or thicket but it may be an undershrub of woods. The leaves are some of the first to be seen in spring, opening in March. They are pale green, entire and oval, about 1·5 in. long, are opposite in growth, turning deep red in autumn. Frequently they hang black on the tree after the first severe frost. The bark (10b) is greenish grey on the bole but red on the thinner branches and twigs. Flowers come in June—July. They are white, 4-petalled (10c) arranged in clusters with an unpleasant smell. Small insects are attracted to them in great numbers. The fruits are small berries which begin green but become black and glossy (10a) in September. The fleshy parts of Dogwood berries are very bitter and inside there are 2 hard seeds. Dogwood suckers freely and may quickly invade unused land or abandoned fields. Despite its small size, the wood is so hard that many uses have been found for it including turnery and tool handles.

11 CORNELIAN CHERRY *Cornus mas* L. 25 ft
12 IVY *Hedera helix* L. 90 ft

11a   **11b**

Despite its name the **Cornelian Cherry** is not a Cherry but a member of the Dogwood family. It is not native, being introduced from the Mediterranean region and widely planted in parks and gardens because of its attractive flowers, fruits and bark. The leaves (11c) are oval, opposite and entire, usually slightly larger than those of Dogwood, but otherwise similar. The flowers (11b) are small and yellow produced in pretty umbels before the leaves expand in February–March. The fruit is a scarlet elliptical berry somewhat like a small cherry — hence the common name of the species. The bark is a warm-brown colour

11c

(11a) rather soft to the touch and tending to flake away from the bole. In a few places in the south of Britain Cornelian Cherry has become naturalised in hedgerows, where the seeds have been dispersed by birds.

Ivy is a native evergreen woody climber that is abundant throughout the British Isles. It is not parasitic on the tree that supports it but its roots compete for nutrients in the soils with those of its host and sometimes it may do serious harm. Often it grows so densely over an old, dead trunk that its dark-green foliage gives the look of an Ivy tree (12a). Other times it will use a wall or any similar support or even trail along the ground. Ivy stems may be up to 10 in. in diameter and are densely covered with adhesive 'roots' with which it climbs into the light to flower wherever opportunity affords. Vegetative shoots and flower shoots are quite different. The former have the leaves arranged in 2 rows. Leaves are palmately veined with whitish veins and are also palmately lobed. On the flowering shoots the leaves grow all round the stem, have only one main vein and are oval and entire. Both types of leaves are a glossy, dark green. The flowering shoots of Ivy do not have climbing 'roots' and cuttings can be taken to produce pleasantly shaped bushes. Flowering starts in September and is often so profuse that the whole flowering shoot is covered with blooms (12c). The flowers are small yellow-green with all parts in fives. The smell, unpleasant to man, of the abundant nectar is extremely attractive to flies and wasps. The fruits (12b) are small berries which remain green for most of the winter but ripen to a bluish black the following spring. Ivy prefers mild winters and flowering shoots may be killed back by frost.

12a

12b

12c

13

14a

The Elm family with its large number of species, sub-species and hybrids is notoriously difficult for even the expert botanist to differentiate. However, **Wych Elm** is the easiest one to separate because it is found mainly in the Highland Zone of Britain, it has a larger leaf than the others, carried on a shorter stalk and its roots do not send up sucker shoots. The bark of Wych Elm is distinctive because it is very smooth and grey till the tree is old but then it becomes brown and deeply networked. The crown is a broad, irregular, multiple dome with branches ending in stout shoots. The leaves are very unequal at the base, 4—7 in. by 2·5—4 in., containing about 17 pairs of veins which lead to the larger teeth, with smaller teeth between. The flowers are tiny dark purple-red, and appear before the leaves in March. The fruit (13) is a large pale-green membrane, 1 in. across with a nutlet in the centre. This species is found growing in wood-lands and is used for boat building, tool handles and turnery work.
Other Elms such as **English Elm** are rarely woodland trees, more often occuring in the

14b

14c

13 WYCH ELM *Ulmus glabra* Huds. 90 ft+

14 ENGLISH ELM *Ulmus procera* Salis. 100 ft

15 DUTCH ELM *Ulmus × hollandica* Mill 100 ft

16 SMOOTH-LEAVED ELM *Ulmus carpinifolia* Gleditsch 85 ft

14d

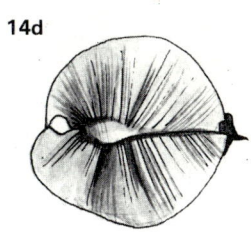

hedgerows. They are very widespread as they tolerate salt and wind and were traditionally used for ship keels and above all, coffin-boards. The English Elm is primarily a tree of the Midlands. It has dark-brown bark (14a) and a conical crown with ascending branches when young. Unfortunately many trees have suffered from Dutch Elm disease in recent years (14c) and have had to be destroyed. The leaves (14b) are dark green, double-toothed with 10–12 pairs of veins. These open early, often in April and may remain green till November, going gold and falling in December. Reproduction is virtually always by suckers, as the fruit (14d) is rarely fertile.

The **Dutch Elm** group are hybrids between Wych Elm and Small-leaved Elm. They have very variable leaves, up to 6 in. by 3 in. (15b), that are smooth above and often have raised teeth.

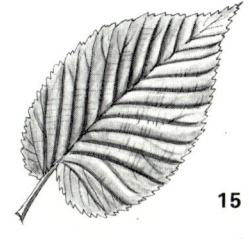

15

The **Smooth-Leaved Elm** has grey-brown bark with deep, long vertical fissures (16c) and thick ridges. The leaves are variable but often elliptic, 3 in. long, with forked veins and very oblique bases (16b). The flowers are red with white stigmas, developing in March, and the fruits are elliptical membranes (16a), smaller than those of the other Elms and with the seed nearer the notch.

16a

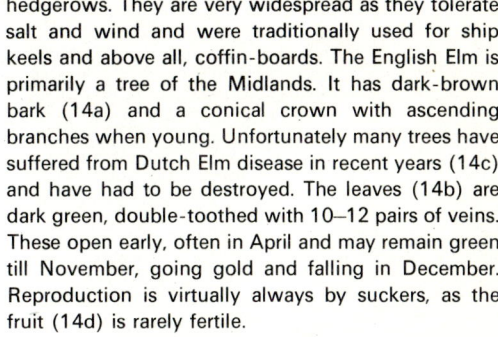
16b

16c

17a   17b

The **Black Mulberry** is the commonest of the two Mulberry trees found in Britain. It is an import from western Asia that was first brought to Britain in the reign of James I and is now found frequently in old-fashioned gardens and parks, mainly in the south of England. The original idea of the introduction was so that the leaves would provide the necessary food for silkworms and in this way save the import of silk from the East. This plan failed because the Mulberry does not grow very quickly in the British climate but the trees continued to be grown for their edible fruit. Most of the very old trees still living probably date back to the original planting. In fact, the Black Mulberry is not the most suitable for rearing silkworms but it is the one that grows best in Britain. The bark is dark orange and there are wide fibrous fissures with frequent sprouts and burrs. Old trees may have their bole virtually buried or leaning and only the low, broad dome visible (17c). Twigs have

short hairs and the buds grow alternately. The leaves are heart-shaped, about 3–4 in. by 3 in. with coarsely toothed edges. They are rough and hairy on both sides with hairs on the veins below. The leaf-stalk is about 1 in. long, stout and hairy. Flowers (17b) arranged in catkins grow in the axils of leaves or at the base of new shoots. There are male and female catkins on the same tree. There is no corolla and a 4-lobed calyx. Male flowers have 4 stamens and the females 2 long white stigmas. The fruit (17a) develops from

17c

17 BLACK MULBERRY, COMMON MULBERRY *Morus nigra* L. 35 ft
18 WHITE MULBERRY *Morus alba* L. 45 ft

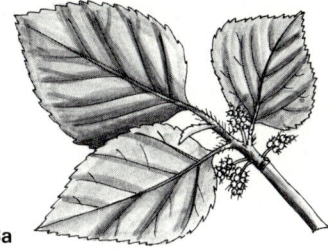

18a

the calyx and the whole mass of flowers on one catkin becomes a compound fruit like a raspberry. This fruit is green in early summer, orange-scarlet by September and then deep blackish red in October. It has a pleasant sub-acid flavour.

White Mulberry is the species pre-ferred by silkworms but it is uncommon in this country. It was first imported towards the end of the seventeenth century and has not been cultivated much out-side specialised gardens. The bark (18c) is a dull grey-green with a shallow pattern of flat, rather wavy ridges. On old trees the bark turns orange-brown. White Mulberry grows tall with a rather narrow crown. The branches are brittle and are often broken. The foliage is rather different from that of the Black Mulberry (18b). The shoots are slender and straight and the leaves rather variable. Some are lobed, others not. Most are partly heart-shaped 4 in. by 3 in. with large triangular teeth. They are smooth and glossy light green, very thin and flat, with a grooved, hairy leaf-stalk. The flowers (18a) are male or female. The females grow on erect, pale-green, cylindrical heads with tiny, black stigmas. The fruit eventually grows like that of the Black Mulberry except that beginning white it then turns yellow, pink or purple. In a very few gardens one may see a weeping variety with very large leaves.

18b

18c

19 FIG *Ficus carica* L. 30 ft
20 WALNUT *Juglans regia* L. 70 ft

19a   19b

The **Fig** is another small tree in the largely tropical Mulberry family. It is very common in England and has been grown here for many centuries. Most Fig trees will be seen growing in urban gardens or parks, usually against a south-facing wall (19b). Sometimes in very sheltered spots they are grown free-standing. Occasionally they will be found self-sown and more or less naturalised in the southern counties but further north the Fig becomes rare. The tree has a rather upswept form and may grow as a bush rather than a true tree. The bark is pale grey and smooth with a pattern of darker grey to black lines. The dark-green leaves are variable in size but usually large, up to 12 in. by 10 in., palmately lobed into 3–5 parts, the middle lobe being always the largest. They are bluntly toothed, rough to the touch above and densely hairy below. The leaf-stalk may be 4 in. in length. The flower is pear-shaped and is pollinated by a gall-wasp. It ripens into an edible fruit 3 in. long (19a). This fruit is small and dark green in the first winter, swelling in the second year then changing through brown to purple. The fruits develop near the tips of growing shoots. The **Walnut** is a native of the area from the eastern Mediterranean to the Far East but it was introduced to Britain in very early times and was known to have been grown in orchards by the Saxons for the sake of its edible nuts. Usually today one finds Walnut as a single tree in farms or cottage gardens but it has also been planted in the wild and spread to more remote hedgerow situations by rooks and other birds fond of the nuts. In Britain it only grows well on rich soils and in high light conditions. Walnut timber is very beautiful and valuable with pale grey-brown sapwood and chocolate heartwood, besides other tints and colours developing in places. It is heavy, hard and fine textured and today is primarily used as a veneer. In the past gun-stocks and quality furniture were made from Walnut. The bark (20d) is grey-green and smooth when young but ages into irregular, flat-surfaced, lenticular ridges. The leaves are extremely large compounded from 7 to 9 leaflets, the largest about 8 in. by 4 in., decreasing in size towards the base of the leaf. They are aromatic, dull yellow-green with yellow veins, leathery and with entire margins. In May–June when they first unfold they are copper coloured. Both sexes of flower grow on the same tree. The males are arranged in thick short catkins which grow on the previous year's shoots (20a), the females are small clusters of yellow-green on new shoots. The fruit (20c) is plum-shaped, green at first, becoming brown and splitting to show the shell beneath. The seed-leaves of the germinating seedling (20b) remain in the shell and the early true leaves have few leaflets.

20a

20b

20c   20d

21 STRAWBERRY-TREE, ARBUTUS *Arbutus unedo* L. 25 ft

22 ASH *Fraxinus excelsior* L. 100 ft+

The **Strawberry-Tree** is our only native tree of the Heather family. It grows wild in the south-west of Ireland from Killarney to Co. Sligo where it forms dense thickets along streamsides, but it is also quite common in village and country gardens elsewhere in southern Ireland and southern Britain. It gets its name from the obvious resemblance of the fruit to strawberries. The evergreen, leathery leaves are simple, alternate and elliptical with sharp, forward-pointing teeth. They are shiny above, pale green beneath with a prominent white midrib. Each leaf is 2–4 in. long, 1–1·5 in. wide. The tree has a very short trunk and a dense, low, rounded head (21a). The bark is dark red at first but on older trees it breaks away

21a

in red-brown flakes. The flowers (21b) are drooping racemes of 15–20 heather-like bells which develop at the end of the new summer's growth and open in autumn and winter. They ripen into 0·5 in. juicy berries which begin white, then turn yellow and finally go pimply red (21c) the next autumn, so that flower and ripe fruit often occur at the same time. These fruits are edible but insipid – hence the Latin name which means 'I eat one' only!

21b

21c

22a

22b

The **Ash** is an abundant, native, tall-domed, often forked, tree (22c) which occurs whenever the soil is base-rich and damp. It is grown as a forest crop on limestone, as part of mixed woodlands elsewhere and also in towns, city parks and around churches. The bark (22a) is often confusing because, when young, it is pale grey and very smooth, much like Beech, but with age it becomes brown and thick, and interwoven ridges develop. It is our last native tree to leaf in May and one of the first to drop its leaves in autumn. In winter it is best recognised by its squat, black, conic buds. The leaves are compound-pinnate 6–9 in. long with 7–15 serrated leaflets, dull green above, paler below with white hair along the midrib. The small variably sexed flowers, coming before the leaves, give the tree a purple look in April. The fruits are the well-known strap-shaped keys (22b) which contain a seed at the base. Some years they remain on the tree throughout the winter. Ash trees may be all male, all female or mixed varying from year to year. Ash timber is still very important for sports equipment and in the past it was a common coppice-crop. **22c**

23a   23b

Manna Ash was imported from the Mediterranean region in the seventeenth century and now occurs frequently in gardens, town parks and as a roadside ornamental, where its smaller size and prettier flowers make it preferable to Ash. The bark (23b) remains very smooth throughout life and is dark grey, often quite black in urban areas. Sometimes they are grafted on to our native Ash stocks and the difference in bark is then very clear. The branches are more twisted than native Ash and the opposite buds are conical and dark brown with grey hairs. The leaves are quite similar to those of Ash but Manna Ash leaflets are less regularly toothed and have 0·5 in. long stalks whereas those of Ash are virtually stalkless. Also the underparts of the leaves have a brown or white woolly covering either side of the veins. The flowers are borne on an inflorescence of about 7 branches. They are creamy white, dense and fragrant. There is less sexual confusion compared with native Ash as the flowers are either wholly male or mixed. The seeds are keys similar to those of common Ash (23a) but rather more slender. They do not germinate until the second year. These two Ashes, Lilac and Privet are all part of the Olive family which also contains many of our better-known garden shrubs.

Lilac can grow into an attractive and robust tree though most people think of it as a

23 MANNA ASH *Fraxinus ornus* L. 60 ft
24 LILAC *Syringa vulgaris* L. 20 ft

shrub of the flower border. There are many garden varieties of this species with flowers all shades. Lilac grows wild in south-east Europe and western Asia but has been cultivated as an ornamental shrub since the Middle Ages. From thence it has become naturalised in hedges, thickets and derelict shrubberies where it often spreads extensively by suckering. The brown rough, fibrous bark (24b) is very distinctive in the way that it peels off in thin flakes. The leaves are opposite, entire, oval to heart-shaped, 2–4 in. across. They are very thin and do not change colour before falling. The flowers of the wild specimens are light violet (24a) or white with the petals united in a tube. They grow in terminal clusters which open in May and June and are very attractive to bees. The fruits are acute, smooth capsules (24c) with narrow, winged seeds 0·5 in. long. The wood of the Lilac has a central pith which is easily removed to produce pipe-like instruments or tools. This was its main use in the past. The wood is heavy and hard with light sapwood and purple heartwood. It is still used today for quality inlay work.

24a **24b**

24c

Wild Privet is a small tree or shrub that is common in hedges and scrubland especially on lime-rich soils. It gets its name from the same root as 'private' because it was so frequently used in the past to enclose private gardens. It is tardily deciduous rather than evergreen and today most hedges are planted with the Japanese Privet, *L. ovalifolium* which has rounder leaves and may be fully evergreen except in dirty urban areas. Wild Privet often forms thickets in the wild, such as in the scrub around the Norfolk Broads, where it suckers and layers over considerable areas. It is also frequent on the Downs. The short-stalked leaves are opposite, lance-shaped and entire, 1–2 in. long, shiny dark green above and light green below. In autumn they turn a violet colour and usually fall by midwinter. Young branches are very slightly hairy and olive-green, later becoming grey. The bark (25c) is smooth and grey-brown. The flowers (25b) are 4-petalled and white with a funnel-shape and very sweet scent. Flowering occurs in June–July in compact panicles, which are visited by a great many insects. The fruits (25a) are small, shiny, black berries which ripen in September–October. They are well-liked by birds and also used for decorative purposes. A larger Privet occasionally seen is the Chinese Privet which is fully evergreen and may grow to 35 ft. It has much larger opposite leaves and winter flowers.

25a

25b

25c

25 WILD PRIVET *Ligustrum vulgare* L. 20 ft
26 SWEET BAY, BAY LAUREL, POET'S LAUREL *Laurus nobilis* 40 ft

26b

26a

26c

Sweet Bay is an aromatic evergreen which was introduced to Britain in the mid-sixteenth century. It is thought that this species was the sacred tree of Apollo, used as the emblem of victory in ancient Greece and especially known from the Olympic Games. Under the Romans too this tree was an important ritual species and even today we talk of the poet 'laureate' and the university 'baccalaureate'. Originally a tree of Asia Minor, Sweet Bay now grows all round the Mediterranean and will thrive in the southern half of Britain. It is often seen as a garden shrub but more rarely will grow to a medium-sized tree. The glossy, dark-green leathery leaves are used in stews and even to flavour some sardines. They are spirally arranged on the tree, 3–4 in. long by 1·5 in. broad, finely crinkled and toothed. The flowers open in late April (26a). They are small and pale yellow, coming in small groups beneath each leaf on very short stalks. Male and female flowers are on separate trees. The male flowers are usually in larger groups, up to five, and have 8–12 stamens. The female flowers normally come in pairs and have only rudimentary stamens. The fruits are tiny, shiny, deep-green eggs that enlarge to 0·5 in. and turn black in autumn (26b). The tree has dark grey-black bark which is smooth when young (26c) but becomes wrinkled with age.

27a

27b

Elder is common in England, Ireland and Wales, but not Scotland. There, an introduced shrub, the Red-Berried Elder, *S. racemosa*, may be seen. Elder grows best in soils rich in nitrogen and occurs as a weed around houses, farms and rabbit burrows. It is one of the few plants that rabbits will not eat and it, therefore, occurs widely on Breck and Down. Usually it grows as a bush but may reach tree proportions if left unattended such as in derelict hedges or as an understory in Ash woods. Annual shoots are green and have many grey lenticels. Older stems become light brown to grey and have an extremely furrowed bark (27b). The yellow-white wood is hard and heavy

27c

with a pithy centre. It is useful for wooden spoons and tool handles. The leaves are compound-pinnate, having 5—7 oval leaflets, 1·5—3·5 in. long, with toothed margins, something like Ash. The profuse blossoms (27c) are composed of clusters of sweet-smelling yellow-white flowers, highly attractive to flies. The fruits, called Elder-berries, are 3—4-seeded drupes, which start green and ripen to blackish violet (27a). Both flower and fruit make excellent wine, and the berries are used in various herbal remedies. Many birds, too, eat the berries and consequently aid dispersal. Elder is usually thought of as a weed tree and its green parts are poisonous. On the other hand it carries leaves through much of the year, unless frost blackens the foliage, and its reproductive parts are an important source of food for many wild creatures.

27 ELDER *Sambucus nigra* L. 25 ft
28 WAYFARING-TREE *Viburnum lantana* L. 20 ft

The **Wayfaring-Tree** was so named by the herbalist Gerard in the sixteenth century because he found it so commonly along the hedges of Drove roads. Today it is most commonly found in chalk and limestone areas but it also occurs on sands and by the south coast. The opposite, oval leaves, 2–4 in. long, are easily identified by their finely toothed margins and white, woolly covering of fine hairs. In autumn the leaves turn deep red. The down extends over the opposite buds and pliable branchlets and is an aid in the conservation of moisture. The Wayfaring-Tree carries large terminal umbels of identical 5-petalled white flowers in June (28a). The flowers are both self-pollinated and pollinated by insects. The fruits are berries 0·3 in. in diameter which ripen through green, yellow, coral and red (28b) to black. They are oval and compressed rather than round. The fruits have a sour smell and taste but are greedily eaten by birds. The bark is heavily fissured in old trees. This species and many of its close relatives are frequently used in decorative shrubberies. In the wild it has spread widely over Downland where rabbits and sheep are excluded.

28a

28b

29 GUELDER-ROSE *Viburnum opulus* L. 20 ft
30 HONEYSUCKLE, WOODBINE *Lonicera periclymenum* L. 20 ft+

29a

Guelder-Rose, Wayfaring-Tree and Elder are all members of the same family. The first is the smallest, rarely reaching 20 ft, but is also the most beautiful (29b). It gets its name from the cultivated race, the Snowball-Tree which comes from Guelderland in the Netherlands. Guelder-Rose is an occasional undershrub of moist woodlands and hedges such as around fens and the Norfolk Broads. The twigs and branches are smooth and angular, greenish grey at first later becoming red-brown. The winterbuds are opposite yellow-green and wrapped in scales. The leaves, too, are opposite and when they open they are covered in down. However, this is lost as the deeply toothed lobes expand. The leaves are up to 3 in. across with 3–5 lobes. In autumn they turn a rich crimson before falling. The flowers come at the end of shoots of the current year, grouped in flat clusters. The outermost ring are showy but sterile; the inner flowers secrete nectar and are fertile. Self-fertilisation and insect pollination occur. The fruits are magnificent flat clusters of scarlet translucent berries (29a) each containing one seed. They are, however, repellent to taste. Often they are too heavy to be held by the twigs so that trees are bowed down by their weight as the leaves turn in the autumn. The seeds are dispersed by birds, especially thrushes and pigeons but do not germinate until the next year.

29b

Although not a tree **Honeysuckle** is included in this booklet, like Ivy, because it is common in woodlands. Honeysuckle is a woody climber which twines round young saplings and constricts them (30b) causing strange corkscrew-like contortions. In this way it is quite a serious forest pest, but when it climbs up a mature tree to flower in the light above, its beautiful, fragrant flowers take on quite a different look. The opposite, elliptical, entire leaves unfold in April, dark green above and blue-green below. The flowers come at the end of shoots in June—July, irregular and funnel-shaped (30a) with a narrow corolla tube 1 in. long. The flowers are red outside and yellow inside. In the evening the scent is very strong and they are fertilised by hawk-moths which can reach the nectar at the base of the tube. The fruits are round, red berries. Honeysuckle grows on most soils throughout Britain but only flowers in the light. The name Honeysuckle comes from the fact that one can suck sweet nectar from the flower.

30a

30b

31 INDIAN BEAN-TREE, CATALPA *Catalpa bignonioides* Walt. 50 ft

31a   31b

The **Indian Bean-Tree** is a handsome tree that was introduced from the U.S.A. in 1726. It is frequently seen in the south of England in parks and gardens and sometimes by roadsides. The finest trees with low, wide-spreading domes (31a) are in Cambridge, Oxford and London. In full flower in late summer it is one of the best trees we possess. The bark is fissured into flat ridges and is usually dull pink and brown (31c). The leaves, which leave large leaf-scars on the shoots, develop in June in whorls of 3 or opposite. They are extremely large, up to 10 in. by 9 in., oval, with a tapered point and indented base. The margins are waved but entire and the impressed veins are hairy below. The gorgeous scented flowers (31b) are in conical panicles 8 in. high with each flower a 2 in. wide bell with a 3-lobed lip and a hood. They are white with brown, red and yellow lines. The fruit is a slender pod up to 15 in. long which may remain on the tree over winter. Unfortunately much of the growth this tree makes in our climate is cut back each year by frost.

31c